Contents

About the Author

Introduction

My Debt Story

A World Built on Debt

Your Debt Payoff, and What to Expect

Debt Payoff Stage 1: Getting Motivated and Adopting the Right Money Mindset

Debt Payoff Motivation

Dealing With Demotivation

The Right Money Mindset

Getting Motivated and Adopting the Right Money Mindset: Five Minute Motivation

Getting Motivated and Adopting the Right Money Mindset: Recap

Debt Payoff Stage 2: Addressing Toxic Debt Behaviour

My Toxic Debt Behaviour

Your Toxic Debt Behaviour

Eliminating the Triggers to Your Toxic Debt Behaviour

If Your Behaviour Isn't Toxic

Addressing Toxic Debt Behaviour: Five Minute Motivation

Addressing Toxic Debt Behaviour: Recap

Debt Payoff Stage 3: Compiling Your Debt List

Debts to Include on Your Debt List

Debts to Exclude From Your Debt List

Your Debt List: The Finer Details

Compiling Your Debt List When You Don't Have All of the Details to Hand

Dealing With a Larger-Than-Expected Debt Total

Coming to Terms With Your Debt Total

Putting Your Debt List Into Order of Repayment

Compiling Your Debt List: Five Minute Motivation

Compiling Your Debt List: Recap

Debt Payoff Stage 4: Building a Budget

How a Budget Can Help You

How Realistic Is Life on a Budget?

The Main Elements of Any Budget

Calculating Your Income

Calculating Your Expenditure

Adding Sinking Funds

Finalising Your Budget

What to Do With Your Discretionary Income

What to Do When Your Discretionary Income Is Zero or in a Deficit

Building Your Budget: Five Minute Motivation

Building a Budget: Recap

Debt Payoff Stage 5: Trimming Your Budget

Trimming Fixed Expenses

Trimming Variable Expenses

A Practical Approach to Trimming Your Budget

An Emotional Approach to Trimming Your Budget

How Much Is Too Much When It Comes to Trimming Your Budget?

Trimming Your Budget: Five Minute Motivation

Trimming Your Budget: Recap

Debt Payoff Stage 6: Increasing Your Income

Using the Right Money Mindset When You Side Hustle

Can't I Just Ask for a Pay Rise or Get a Better-Paid Job?

Do I Have to Side Hustle?

The Importance of Not Burning Out

Choosing the Right Side Hustle

Side Hustle Ideas

Increasing Your Income: Five Minute Motivation

Increasing Your Income: Recap

Debt Payoff Stage 7: Saving for Emergencies

What Do Emergency Savings Cover?

How Much Should My Emergency Savings Be?

Funding Emergency Savings When You Already Have Savings

Where to Keep Your Emergency Savings

How Do I Start to Save for Emergencies?

Saving for Emergencies: Five Minute Motivation

Saving for Emergencies: Recap

Debt Payoff Stage 8: Overpaying Debt

Figuring Out Your Debt-Free Date

Paying Off Debt Is a Marathon, Not a Sprint

Overpaying Debt: Five Minute Motivation

Overpaying Debt: Recap

Life After Debt

Where Do You Go From Here?

Debt Payoff FAQs

Acknowledgements

Copyright

About the Author

Grainne McNamee gave herself a goal in July 2017: to pay off £16,000 of debt in one year. With no idea how she was going to achieve her goal, she started immersing herself in personal finance; mastering budgeting, figuring out ways to decrease her expenses and learning how to increase her income. Most importantly, she came up with a fool proof method for getting out of debt, which this book comprises.

But that was just the beginning. Having achieved debt freedom, Grainne now runs WannaBeDebtFree, which aims to help people in the UK get out of debt and live their best financial lives. She has appeared in many publications such as The Daily Mail and The Daily Mirror talking about her debt free lifestyle and encouraging others to improve their mindset around their finances.

In addition to her blog, Grainne can usually be found on Instagram and TikTok, posting about food, mental health, and wellbeing from a financial perspective.

Introduction

How do you feel when you think about money?

You might feel secure, organised and on top of your finances. You're aware of your total debt and savings. As for planning, you have long-term financial goals that you're working towards, and you know your net worth and how much you can comfortably afford to spend each month.

Or, every time you think about money, you feel full of dread. You're anxious when you open your bank statements and avoid online banking so you don't have to face the situation. You worry about how you'll pay your bills. Perhaps you argue with your partner about money. Meanwhile, you find yourself impulse buying and making purchases you can't afford. Debt affects your sleep, your well-being, your relationships and your happiness. You don't have your finances in order.

If you're in the latter category, then let me tell you: *it's going to be ok*. Your finances and your future are fixable. And that's where this book comes in; it's going to help you with your debt payoff and fix your money mindset for good.

My Debt Story

I know what it's like to be in debt; that recklessness when it comes to purchasing, coupled with the feelings of dread and anxiety when my credit card statements came in.

A few years ago, my partner and I were living beyond our means. We had recently purchased a new car (financed through the dealership – ouch!) for £11,000. We had also just bought our first home, which we renovated, getting us £13,000 further into a financial hole.

Despite our shiny surface, we were drowning. Not only in debt, but in the stress of repayments and living beyond our means, which were taking their toll on our health and well-being. The more we acquired, the less we could afford. The less money we had, the more money became the focal point of our lives.

By July 2017, unable to recognise the lives we had built for ourselves, we realised that we needed to change the way we managed our money. We set ourselves a goal to pay off our debt in one year.

What happened over that year was life changing. We learned to budget and live below our means without sacrificing our quality of life. In fact, many aspects of our lives were enhanced when we started to strip back everything that we were wasting money on and see what was truly important underneath that shiny surface.

We paid off our debt two days before our target date. As well as regaining our financial future, we found choices, happiness, better mental health and peace. Getting out of debt was, hands down, the best money we've ever spent.

However, even though our lives have changed, the world around us hasn't. If anything, the world is hurtling towards a consumer debt crisis at an unprecedented rate. But it doesn't have to be that way. You *can* be debt-free and live better for less.

But when did being in debt become the norm?

A World Built on Debt

Everyone has their own financial story to tell, and it's becoming increasingly common to hear tales of debt, despair and defaulting payments among the people we know. We live in a world of expensive technology, which connects us through social media – one of the biggest motivators that many of us have for getting into debt.

Our generation is unique in that we are the first to get a glimpse into the carefully curated lives of friends, family, strangers and celebrities via social media. The pressure to "keep up" is immense.

Of course, that's just one factor in the melting pot of consumer debt.

We also have higher house prices and less job security than our parents did. We are in the midst of a cost of living crisis, and many of us are still exhibiting the behaviours of pre-2008 recession times – relying on credit instead of savings, financing and refinancing everything we "own", and emulating the behaviour of older generations that enjoyed an equity boom, when we are in a completely different, and disadvantaged, position.

In today's world, not only is it common to turn to debt as a means of purchasing whatever you want, it's *expected*.

If you want a new car, you can just walk into a dealership and take one home that day, albeit by signing a few forms that commit you to a huge sum of money, plus interest, over the course of the next few years of your life. But none of that matters when you have that shiny new car (until you have to make the repayments, of course).

If you want a new outfit, you can sign up for store credit and buy what you want without having to pay a penny right now, although you need to enter into a legally binding contract to pay a huge rate of interest on your purchases. But again, none of that matters when you have that perfect purchase that's going to change your life (until you have to make the repayments, of course).

If you are short on cash, you can log on to a website and apply for a short-term loan to tide you over until payday. On payday, you can pay it back at an astronomical interest rate, meaning you'll be more likely to keep borrowing in the run-up to your next payday. But none of that matters because you've got the money in your account now (until you have to make the repayments, of course).

If you really think about all of the ways that we can acquire debt, how easy it is to purchase anything we want, and the extent to which marketing is shoved in our faces daily, debt may seem inevitable for many people.

However, does that mean that a lifetime in debt is *your* fate?

No! Absolutely not.

Don't condition yourself to the idea that you'll forever be parting with huge chunks of your income to pay for your debt.

Don't entertain the thought that you have to accept the mental and physical toll debt takes on you.

Don't accept that your financial fate can be determined by people whose job it is to extract as much money from you as possible.

Ultimately, you are in control of your finances. You can decide right now to make better choices, follow a plan and create a better relationship with your money. As long as you understand what you can afford, debt doesn't have to be your fate.

In fact, armed with some basic budgeting skills, planning, motivation and the right money mindset, you can get out of debt and build a brighter financial future.

Your Debt Payoff, and What to Expect

Your debt payoff plan will consist of eight stages:

1. Getting motivated and adopting the right money mindset
2. Addressing toxic debt behaviour
3. Compiling a debt list
4. Building a budget
5. Trimming your budget
6. Increasing your income
7. Saving for emergencies
8. Overpaying debt

In this book, you are going to learn how to pay off your unsecured consumer debt (credit cards, loans, car finance, etc.). This strategy is what is referred to throughout this book as your *debt payoff*.

The reason your debt payoff focuses on unsecured consumer debt only is because this provides a manageable challenge to tackle while you start to make changes to the way you handle your finances.

Once you complete your debt payoff, you can move on to applying the same strategy to tackling larger debts such as your mortgage or student loans, if you wish.

As part of your debt payoff plan, you will aim to get rid of your monthly debt repayments, reduce your expenditure and increase your income. Therefore, this will turn your financial difficulty into financial prosperity.

Getting out of debt may seem like a straightforward exercise of making repayments, but it's so much more than that. Like any goal, long-term success is all in the journey. So instead of focusing merely on repayments, we are going to start by delving into motivation and get you into the right money mindset, so that you'll be able to stay focused even when your motivation wanes.

We'll also work on addressing any toxic debt behaviour you may have that is keeping you tethered to debt.

As for taking action against your debts, you will then compile a list of what you owe. You'll gather key information that will help you to start your debt payoff by deciding the order in which you tackle your debt.

Then you'll build a budget. The first budget you put together on your debt payoff will give you an insight into where you were previously going wrong with your money. From here, you'll be working consistently over the course of your debt payoff to reduce your expenses in the areas that you can.

You'll also find a way to increase your income by taking on a side hustle that suits your circumstances.

Once you start using and sticking to your budget, you will start to see your finances improve immediately.

By using your budget, you are going to figure out how much discretionary income you have. With your discretionary income, you will save some money for emergencies. These emergency savings are important as, because you'll no longer be relying on debt, you'll need a savings fund in case anything goes wrong during your debt payoff.

Then with your emergency savings in place, you are going to overpay debt until you are debt-free. Making these overpayments is likely to be the longest part of the journey.

While you're making overpayments, you'll also continue to work on cutting your expenses month-on-month and increasing your income.

You will find throughout your debt payoff that you will be working on various stages at once. You'll have to remain motivated, focused on the right money mindset and committed to addressing and fixing toxic debt behaviour throughout. When it comes to building your budget, you'll be working on trimming your budgetary expenses and increasing your income as you save and pay off debt.

Combining the actions of some stages, alongside working on improving your mindset, making good choices and improving your situation, will be the recipe for success to your debt payoff.

During each stage, you will have the opportunity to complete a short motivational exercise, known as *Five Minute Motivation*. These are little tasks to get you into the right money mindset and fired up to smash your goals.

To get motivated to start your debt payoff, how would your finances look if you had no debt repayments to make, plus lower expenses than you currently have *and* a higher income?

With that idea in mind, let's begin.

Debt Payoff Stage 1: Getting Motivated and Adopting the Right Money Mindset

When it comes to paying off debt, motivation and mindset are *everything*.

Starting your debt payoff journey requires motivation, but to carry yourself through the tough times and continue practising good financial habits when you are debt-free, you need the *right money mindset*.

Throughout your debt payoff, both work in conjunction with each other; motivation keeps you enthused and energetic despite the tough demands of your debt payoff, and mindset helps you to focus on taking the right actions and making good decisions.

In this chapter, you are going to focus on motivation and mindset to give you the best possible start to your debt payoff journey and every chance of success in achieving your goal of debt freedom.

Debt Payoff Motivation

Right now, it is likely that you are sick of your monthly salary getting eaten up by debt repayments.

You dread the thought of working another day, knowing how much of your efforts are going straight to debt and interest.

You're tired of being broke all the time and never feeling like you have anything to show for all of your hard work.

You are frustrated by how little money you have to enjoy life with.

You feel frustrated at the stress you're under, the lack of peaceful sleep you get and arguing about money with your partner.

More than anything, you want to be debt-free, and even though everyone around you might be telling you that debt is normal, inevitable or an expectation in modern life, you don't believe them. For you, a life in constant debt is a life not worth carrying on for.

So you're pumped to get started with your debt payoff: you know it's going to be hard but you're still excited to begin. That's motivation, and it is absolutely the best thing you can harness in getting started on your debt payoff – even more than a salary increase.

Motivation is what the start of your debt payoff is fuelled by. In later chapters, you'll put together a budget, start allocating more money to debt and even pick up some extra income, and you need the motivation to carry you through all of those things.

Each step of the way in this book, you will complete a Five Minute Motivation exercise, and you need to build on this by constantly reminding yourself of the reasons you're paying off your debt. Throughout your debt payoff, it's not only important to actually make those overpayments but to reflect upon your progress every step of the way and celebrate your achievements.

It's important that you build a system of rewards for each little milestone you reach on your journey. For example, every time you pay off a debt, do something to mark the occasion, like toast your progress with a bottle of champagne, take a road trip or have a big slice of cake.

Yes, these things cost money, but these expenses are such a tiny part of your overall financial picture and they mean so much when you are working hard and sacrificing during your debt payoff, so put them in your budget. Of course, you can always do something free that marks the occasion if you wish.

The purpose of celebrating the little things is not just to give you an incentive to keep going and to mark the occasion with something special, but ultimately to refresh you on this long journey to debt freedom. Like a marathon runner may need to quench their thirst with water, you, too, need to pause along the way and take a breather. Once you restart after pausing, you will feel ready to go again.

As well as celebrating all of your mini-milestones, I want you to reflect upon the life improvements that your debt payoff triggers on a daily basis to help you when you're struggling. These little reflections will serve as a reminder of what this process is adding to your life in addition to less debt, and you can call on them at times where you feel like giving up.

Pay attention to the little things that spark happiness in your life that you can link back to your debt payoff and see them as short-term rewards for your efforts.

Here are just some benefits you can expect to reap, to get an idea of life improvements to look out for:

- ☐ Less time wasted on unfulfilling activities such as shopping or social media scrolling, therefore more time to focus on fulfilling activities.

- Less focus on seeking happiness from external sources and more introspective focus on happiness.

- Fewer funds available for unhealthy takeaways and ready meals and more funds available for healthier home cooking.

- Less opportunity for toxic debt behaviour and more opportunity for growth.

It's important to take note when you realise you're experiencing any benefits. As your debt payoff might be a long-term goal, these benefits will immediately reward your hard work. They will carry you through the hard times when the road feels long.

Dealing With Demotivation

Let's face it, demotivation is inevitable. Despite the instant rewards and the financial freedom at the end of your debt payoff journey, there will be times when you feel demotivated. There might even be times where you go backwards and slip back into debt.

There is no shame in slipping up or feeling demotivated. We are all human, we all get demotivated, and it's hard to completely overhaul your life without the occasional bump in the road. The key to progress is to accept that there will be times where you will get demotivated or temporarily fall back into an old pattern.

It's not the problems you encounter along your debt payoff journey, but how you deal with them that dictates your success.

For example, let's say you drop your mobile phone, and it causes a tiny crack at the edge of the handset, but it's still perfectly useable, despite the tiny flaw. What would you do? Would you leave it on the ground and continue to stamp on it until it's damaged beyond repair?

Of course you wouldn't! You'd lift it up and thank your lucky stars that the damage is minimal, of course.

Apply this analogy to money. If you slip up and exceed your budget or use your credit card, see it as a lesson learned and move on. No berating yourself, creating destructive thoughts or self-sabotage. Realise you made a mistake – which can also be a learning opportunity by figuring out the trigger that led you there – and start again.

(This idea does rely on self-honesty. If you find that your slip-ups cost more than you're paying off, you need to identify your toxic debt behaviour, which we will explore during the next stage of your debt payoff.)

Your debt payoff can feel long and arduous at times – trust me on this. As much as you might get joy from reduced stress, achieving your goals or discovering a simpler life under your former layers of monetary distractions, there are going to be times when you'll want to quit because you're demotivated.

And that's why you need the *right money mindset*.

The Right Money Mindset

To adopt the right mindset during your debt payoff, you need to shift your focus from your current priorities that led you into debt to new priorities that lead you out of debt.

When we talk about mindset, there are two elements: fuel and outcome. Mindset fuel motivates you to think a certain way, and the outcome is what happens in your life as a result of that fuel.

We get into debt by having the wrong money mindset, meaning that our mindset is fuelled by things that are ultimately financially fruitless, or won't deliver the outcomes you expect them to. Here are some examples of common wrong money mindsets:

- ☐ Being fuelled by trying to keep up appearances on social media, only to feel fraudulent.

- ☐ Being fuelled by the opinions of others and getting into debt by trying to gain their approval or curating your ideal image, only to realise that pandering to the opinions of others negates self-confidence.

- ☐ Being fuelled by low self-esteem and getting into debt by buying products that promise to fix this, only to realise that by doing so you are reinforcing the idea that you are deficient.

- ☐ Being fuelled by feeling overwhelmed by the many influences and demands in your life and getting into debt by not having clarity over what you need to buy and what you don't.

Think of how you got into debt in the first place. How was your money mindset wrong, and could you have done anything differently?

So what about the right money mindset? You need to choose fuel with an outcome where you have a better relationship with money, and there are a lot of specifics under that broad spectrum that you can apply to this, such as:

- ☐ Being fuelled by getting out of debt.
- ☐ Being fuelled by having savings.
- ☐ Being fuelled by paying off your mortgage.
- ☐ Being fuelled by putting your needs first, and luxuries second.
- ☐ Being fuelled by building wealth.
- ☐ Being fuelled by having options.
- ☐ Being fuelled by having a passive income.

When you change your current mindset by fuelling it with something different, your actions will align.

For example, let's say your debt was accrued by making financial decisions based on the opinions of others rather than what you want, and therefore you previously lived beyond your means to keep up a certain lifestyle.

If you adopt the right money mindset by being fuelled by wanting to get out of debt, your focus shifts. Suddenly, you start to become aware of toxic debt behaviour that's going to sabotage your goal, and where you previously purchased mindlessly, you start to become mindful of how you purchase.

Over time, that awareness and mindset shift start to encourage new decisions, new patterns and new outcomes.

So with an idea of what fuelled your wrong money mindset, choose a fuel for the right money mindset and apply your focus to it when you can, particularly at trigger moments, such as when you are about to spend.

It might take some time for your mindset to shift but giving it your focus is the key to achieving the change.

Even when your motivation wanes, the right money mindset will keep your debt payoff going by giving you the fuel to make the right financial decisions. So instead of spending on credit when you're demotivated, you'll take a different course of action, because spending on credit won't get you to your goal.

Adopting the right money mindset is essential if you want the behaviour you learn over the course of your debt payoff to continue long after you finish paying off debt. It is a learned behaviour that is well worth the mental investment.

Getting Motivated and Adopting the Right Money Mindset: Five Minute Motivation

Here is your first Five Minute Motivation to help you start to shift your focus to the right money mindset. Grab a pen and paper and let's get started.

- Decide on three things you want to achieve as a result your debt payoff, other than debt freedom.
  For example, you might like less stress, better well-being or to reduce the amounts of arguments with your partner. If you're stuck, think of what led you to take action against your debts by reading this book.

Take note of them (you can also revisit them during the course of your debt payoff to see if you're making progress on them).

- Write down the fuel to your wrong money mindset and what you think your resulting debt figure is. You are going to work on shifting this throughout the course of your debt payoff, and beyond.

- Choose three goals that will fuel your right money mindset.
Write them down and keep them somewhere that you'll keep seeing them, such as by making them your phone screensaver, or keeping them on the front of your fridge, which will help keep them at the forefront of your mind and start to shift your mindset.

Getting Motivated and Adopting the Right Money Mindset: Recap

In this chapter, we've covered motivation and how to get into the right money mindset, both of which are going to help you to successfully complete your debt payoff. We've also explored demotivation and how to deal with it.

Getting into the right money mindset is crucial when you're tackling debt as it will enable you to keep going, even when your motivation wanes. The right headspace will make all the difference during your debt payoff.

Debt Payoff Stage 2: Addressing Toxic Debt Behaviour

Your debt payoff provides an opportunity to learn from your past spending mistakes and habits. As your payoff progresses, you will identify the toxic debt behaviour that led you into debt. We are able to pinpoint *how* we got into debt easily. We can identify that a car purchase, a designer bag or a new sofa was paid for with credit and we cite this as the reason we are in debt.

However, these are merely our debt in physical format, but they aren't the reason we got into debt; our debt is usually the result of toxic debt behaviour. We are doomed to repeat these patterns until we actually examine and fix the underlying cause.

So if you're paying off debt and not addressing your toxic debt behaviour, you're missing the opportunity to learn from your mistakes and form a better relationship with money. And of course, you stand to gain a lot of fulfilment in being able to give yourself what you actually crave that's fuelling these habits.

In this chapter, you will try to figure out how you got into debt in the first place and examine the root of these feelings. This will help you not only to pay off your debt by eliminating these habits, but you'll be a lot less likely in the future to repeat the cycle and feel more fulfilled as a result.

My Toxic Debt Behaviour

I got into debt when I purchased a new car that I couldn't afford to buy outright and borrowed money to complete a home renovation project. These events led me into debt, but there was an underlying issue that triggered these bad financial decisions.

I got little joy from my day-to-day life, repeating a daily pattern of work, stress, eat, repeat. A lot of my downtime was spent on social media, comparing my life to others and feeling inadequate. I neglected my health, both mental and physical.

The more I ignored the warning signs, the louder they shouted. The only thing I achieved every month was my salary, which I kept investing in the very lifestyle that was making me miserable.

While my life looked great on the outside, I had lost my authentic self under my purchases and was trapped in a cycle of having to earn enough money to pay for my debt, while getting further into debt each month.

I was in the wrong money mindset, fuelled by creating the life I thought others' expected of me, trying to keep up a pretence on social media and following the herd.

When I started my debt payoff, I realised that what had led me into debt wasn't merely poor financial decisions and living beyond my means; debt was an inevitability as long as I was choosing a life path that made me miserable. I compensated for unhappiness with materiality, which only led to more misery and debt.

Completing my debt payoff meant that I found myself with fewer bills to pay and more choices available to me, and I found happiness again. I fuelled my right money mindset with the pursuit of better mental health, happiness and financial freedom.

However, had I paid off my debt without addressing the root cause, I may have found myself back in debt in the future because I didn't understand where I was going wrong.

My story is very relatable among adults today. We strive for misguided goals that we believe will complete us in some way, and often they don't deliver. We pay for expensive housing, new cars and shiny lifestyles, believing that this will enhance our experience of living, when in fact, we mount up debt and reduce our quality of life. As a result, we become trapped in our cycle of work and debt, which then leads to a decrease in happiness, well-being and fulfilment.

Let's examine your own toxic debt behaviour.

Your Toxic Debt Behaviour

What led you into debt?

A short question that throws up a mountain of other questions. However, it is really important that you understand your money habits. There are many common reasons that lead us into debt, for example:

Low self-esteem

- ☐ Buying confidence
- ☐ Curating a version of ourselves for the benefit of others
- ☐ Compensating for never feeling "good enough"

- Affiliating ourselves with certain brands or expensive products that gives us a temporary boost.

Poor health

- Purchasing as a pick-me-up when we are feeling low
- Compensating for poor health with purchases.

Bad money management

- Being unable to possess unallocated money without spending it as soon as possible
- Inability to stick to a budget due to lack of organisation, planning or awareness
- Feeling uncomfortable with saving money.

Unrealistic expectations of purchases

- Believing that the next purchase is going to magically fix our lives
- Needing the feel the "high" of a purchase.

External pressures

- ☐ Having family who rely on us to fund their financial habits, or who have unrealistic expectations of *our* role in *their* finances

- ☐ Trying to keep up a lifestyle that we can't afford

- ☐ Being influenced by social media.

Only you will know the true reasons that you spend and figuring this out requires honest introspection.

However, you owe it to yourself to do this. You deserve the answers that will allow you to give yourself what you really crave.

The root cause of your debt needs to be fixed to be able to achieve the right money mindset. Your debt payoff will get you out of debt but addressing toxic debt behaviour will enable you to sustain real, genuine satisfaction without the urge to buy, and that's priceless.

Eliminating the Triggers to Your Toxic Debt Behaviour

Here are a few techniques that will reduce your exposure to toxic debt situations:

- Unsubscribe from mailing lists and promotional sales emails to avoid being tempted into impromptu purchases.

- Leave your debit and credit cards at home and only carry the cash you need to ensure you don't overspend.

- Change your routine where it leads you into contact with spending opportunities.

- Delete and no longer store your purchase card information on online profiles, which will make it harder to buy impulsively online.

- Change your social media habits, switch off more frequently and unfollow accounts that make you feel inadequate or sell products to you that you don't need, to limit your exposure to esteem-damaging influences.

The mental techniques that you must adopt to overcome your toxic debt behaviour will be specific to you and can only be devised when you become aware of your toxic debt behaviour. You will work on identifying this in this chapter's Five Minute Motivation.

If Your Behaviour Isn't Toxic

What if you believe that your debt is not the result of toxic debt behaviour, and merely just down to the rising cost of living?

As long as you're being honest with yourself, that's fine. Many of us find that we cannot make ends meet no matter how hard we try, and debt is not a choice, but an inevitability.

Debt is encouraged and accepted in our modern society. No money? No problem! Just refinance, remortgage and repeat.

Many of us are living beyond our means because the cost of living continues to gallop ahead of our earnings. We cannot afford to exist in the world we live in. We borrow several times our income and sign away years of our lives, to afford the roof over our heads.

Social media dictates the expectation of living standards. We are encouraged to upgrade as soon as a newer version comes along. We wonder how everyone around us is able to afford their lifestyle while ours is built on mounting debt.

If you identify, don't ignore those alarm bells. Debt is normal, but that doesn't make it a good concept.

You might not have any toxic debt behaviour, so your right money mindset is going to be fuelled by finding a way to live within your means, whether that's through cutting your expenses, upping your income, or both.

Addressing Toxic Debt Behaviour: Five Minute Motivation

In this exercise, we are going to examine the root cause of your debt to identify any potential toxic debt behaviour, so grab and pen and paper and let's get started.

- ☐ List each of your debts (you don't need to know the exact totals just yet). Where your debt is generic, list what you bought with it.
  For example, if you have a few credit cards, make a short list of what you bought with each credit card.

- ☐ Think back to when you bought these items or took out each debt, and what persuaded you to make the decision to buy on credit. Think about:

  - ☐ Influences, such as trying to recreate a lifestyle on social media

  - ☐ Pressures you felt

  - ☐ Your motive underneath the purchase

- Your motivation and focus at the time of the purchase

- What you were trying to achieve by purchasing.

- Think about what you wanted from some of your debt purchases when you bought them. Was it happiness, confidence, inner peace or something else?
Make this the fuel to your right money mindset to start focusing on the solution to your needs.

Addressing Toxic Debt Behaviour: Recap

In this chapter, we've examined toxic debt behaviour and looked at the reason for your underlying debt. This will enable growth and awareness of any issues you have and help to fix any potential lapses, during both your debt payoff and afterwards.

If your debt has been triggered by living beyond your means out of necessity rather than toxic debt behaviour, we will work on budgeting later, which will help to fix the deficit that is causing your debt.

Toxic debt behaviour should be taken seriously, as without it, you might not have debt to deal with.

In fixing the underlying cause, you can not only guarantee yourself a future free from debt, but really get what you need to be happy and fulfilled underneath the layers of materiality.

Debt Payoff Stage 3: Compiling Your Debt List

By compiling your debt list, you will get a wholly accurate picture of what you owe.

A debt list is a list of your debts, plus the details that enable you to put them into the order to tackle them in, and your debt total.

Finding out your exact debt total can be a difficult part of your journey because it forces you to face the reality of the situation. However, facing reality enables you to take positive action when you know the full extent of your debt. It's a tough, but necessary, part of your journey.

So grab a pen and paper and start compiling your debt list. During your debt payoff, your debt list will be your progress indicator and you are going to make it your goal to turn that list into a clean sheet.

Debts to Include on Your Debt List

- ☐ Credit card balances
- ☐ Loan balances
- ☐ Payday loan balances

- Overdraft balances

- Store card/catalogue/store financing balances

- Car finance balances

- Any arrears, such as those for mortgages, council tax, etc.

- Money you owe to family/friends, etc.

Debts to Exclude From Your Debt List

- Your mortgage (which you can tackle after your debt payoff is complete, if you wish)

- Student loans (again, you can tackle these after your debt payoff is complete, if you wish).

However, this is just a guide. If adding any debts to this list will give you comfort, do it.

Your Debt List: The Finer Details

Once you've listed every debt on your debt list, take each debt and note the following details beside it:

- Type of debt (e.g. credit card/loan/overdraft, etc.)

- Name of lender

- Total balance owed right now, to the last penny

- Minimum monthly repayment, to the last penny

- Annual Percentage Rate (APR)

- Any due dates, where applicable (for example, in the case of payday loans, they might be due for repayment by a certain date. You might find that many of your debts do not have a due date, such as in the case of credit cards.)

As part of your debt payoff plan, you will decide the order in which you are going to repay your debts. Your debt list will help you when it comes to choosing the order in which to tackle your overall total.

Compiling Your Debt List When You Don't Have All of the Details to Hand

Your debt list needs to be specific when it comes to each debt; the finer detail is really important. That said, you can compile an outline of your debt list with the information you know, and then fill in the blanks by checking bank statements and contacting lenders when you identify the information you need.

It's always a little bit more difficult to get started when you don't know the specifics of your debts. You may find it overwhelming to take control of your finances when you've previously put off this task and have to face the reality of your debt for the first time.

Many of us don't want to come to terms with our debt total or only have a rough idea of the total, because knowing exactly how much we owe and the full extent of the problem makes your debt "real".

However, whether you calculate your total or not, you are still going to be in the same amount of debt, and only when you know the extent of your debt can you actually take control of the situation and take steps to change it.

Dealing With a Larger-Than-Expected Debt Total

If this has happened to you, never fear; it's very common. Frequently, we tend to forget about a debt or two when all of the information is stored in your head, or the total is miscalculated based on rough figures.

Before deciding to take control of your finances, you might have minimised your debt by rounding down or underestimating the totals. When you aren't taking proactive steps to fix your finances, telling yourself they are minimal can soothe the anxiety they trigger.

In a situation where you've learned that the problem is worse than you had anticipated, you may feel that the issue was better left alone.

You might have convinced yourself that it's easier to bury your head in the sand by not knowing your exact debt total, particularly when your total is higher than expected. Ignore these thoughts. Remember this is a stride forward, not a step back. This is the highest your debt is ever going to be.

Coming to Terms With Your Debt Total

Whether your debt total is a shock or not, now is the time to consider the positives of the situation:

- Now you know exactly how much you owe.
- You can now start to take action.
- As long as you don't continue to spend, your debt total cannot increase.
- This is the turning point in which everything gets better.

There is no debt that cannot be repaid. See your debt as a bundle of stress, and here you are, finally unpacking that bundle and putting it into a comprehensive debt payoff plan. Often, the reason that we don't take positive action sooner is that we don't believe our debt is fixable, but it is.

However, here's a truth bomb:

- Will your debt payoff be uncomfortable at times? Yes.
- Will your debt payoff require a change in behaviour? Of course.

- Will your debt payoff mean sacrificing some future purchases? Yep!

This is as bad as paying off debt gets. And the pay off at the end of your debt payoff? *So* worth it.

It's vital that you don't feel disheartened by your debt total. The right money mindset is key to your debt payoff and getting disheartened will set you back. Therefore, you need to focus on the solution rather than the problem. It's normal to feel sad, annoyed or frustrated, but remember that you can't change the past, but you *can* learn from your mistakes and take positive action to rectify the problem.

Now that you know your debt total, you are empowered to start paying off debt.

Putting Your Debt List Into Order of Repayment

Now that you've compiled a list of all of your debts, you need to put your debt list into the order in which you are going to pay off each debt.

How you pay off your debts is a personal choice which needs to be based on your own circumstances. Here are your options:

- Repayment Option #1: Motivation – Smallest Debt to Largest Debt

By paying off your debts by the smallest amount to largest, you'll get motivation in spades at the beginning of your debt payoff. When your goal is debt freedom, the boost you will get from knocking out those smaller debts in your first few months will really help to carry you on when your motivation is low.

A potential downside is that this option may cost you more over the duration of your debt payoff as interest charges aren't taken into account.

It is up to you how much motivation is worth to you, and I think that this is a great option if you need that extra push to complete your debt payoff.

- Repayment Option #2: Smart – Largest APR to Smallest

In tackling your debt payoff by largest APR to smallest, you pay off your debts in order of interest expense, therefore helping you to save money by eliminating your most expensive debts first.

An added bonus is that the money you save can, in turn, be used to pay off debt, and therefore help you get out of debt quicker.

In particular, if you have a few 0% interest deals that aren't due to expire before the end of your projected debt-free date, it makes financial sense to leave these until after high APR debts have been paid off.

However, your debt payoff requires motivation, and progress may seem slow in the beginning, particularly if you are tackling a large debt first. Regardless, the smart option is for those who are using their debt payoff to begin forming new habits with money, and a little bit of delayed gratification never hurt anyone.

- Repayment Option #3: Priority – Perceived Most Urgent to Least Urgent

This option is for those whose well-being is being affected by debt, particularly when they can pinpoint debts that stress them out more than others.

During my own debt payoff, I chose this option, prioritising my debts by paying off what was most urgent to me.

My car finance deal was due to expire, and it was stressing me out. I had the option to pay several thousand pounds to the car finance company in order to keep my car, or hand it back to the dealership and purchase another car (potentially getting locked into more debt to buy a used car).

In both scenarios, I felt that I was going backwards, and felt demotivated to start my debt payoff. As a result, I chose to focus on my car debt first. This meant for the short-term sacrifice of paying that money, I was able to keep my car and get rid of a monthly car payment.

The priority option can potentially mean paying more in interest or seeing slow progress, but when a particular debt is stressing you out more than the others, it may benefit you more over the course of your debt payoff to make this a priority.

So whether you opt for Motivation, Smart or Priority as your repayment order, consider which of these options best fits your circumstances. Once decided, you can structure your list accordingly.

Compiling Your Debt List: Five Minute Motivation

Now that you've compiled your debt list, let's take five minutes to get motivated.

For this exercise, total up your monthly minimum repayments to figure out just how much you're paying towards debt each month, and use this figure to complete the following:

- Divide your total monthly minimum debt repayment figure by your total monthly take-home income, and multiply by 100. This is the percentage of your monthly income that is taken up by debt.

- Divide your total monthly minimum debt repayments by your hourly rate of pay (which you can estimate if you don't have it to hand). This is how many hours you are working each month to afford to pay the minimum repayments on your debt.

Then ask yourself:

- What are you paying for when you pay your minimum monthly repayments; things that you use, or unnecessary purchases?

- [ ] What would you be able to do with that money instead?

- [ ] How would having that money in your pocket each month affect your quality of life?

- [ ] Are you losing out in order to pay this money?

- [ ] Are you sacrificing time with family, friends and loved ones to earn the money to service these debts?

- [ ] Have you neglected self-care – through physical health, mental health or even just happiness – as a result of your debt?

- [ ] Would you be able to service these debts if your income dropped?

- [ ] Is there a better use of this money, or the time you spend earning this money?

If any of your answers indicate that your debt is not servicing a necessity in your life, then this is your cue to change.

If your debt derives from toxic debt behaviour or living beyond your means, then your debt payoff serves as a great opportunity to rewrite your financial future and form better money habits.

If your answers have helped you to realise that you are losing out as a result of your debt (for example, you're sacrificing time with loved ones to afford to service your debt, or you are stuck in a particular job that you dislike in order to meet your minimum monthly repayments), then you need to use this as fuel to carry you to the end of your debt payoff.

Compiling Your Debt List: Recap

By now, you will have completed your debt list, you know your exact debt total and you've decided the order in which you are going to pay off your debt.

Right now, your debt is the highest it will ever be, and things can only get better from here.

Debt Payoff Stage 4: Building a Budget

Regardless of income, *everyone* needs a budget. Building financial security depends on what you spend, *not* what you earn.

Take a second to digest that; it is the single best piece of advice I could give you about money, yet it is so seldom applied.

Culturally, we think that the more money we have, the better off we are financially. However, we need to take our expenditure into account to get an accurate picture of our financial health.

Many of us focus on the idea that increasing our income is the answer to our financial problems, and we chase money as the solution. Whether your goal is to get out of debt, have savings, achieve a better quality of life, be happy or even just to have some form of security, we believe more money is the answer.

And it can be a contributor, as long as your spending doesn't exceed your earnings. But money alone is not the solution, because you need to adopt the right money mindset in order to manage your money well in the long-term. Therefore, having more money won't improve your finances if you're spending more than you earn.

You have a much better chance of getting out of debt by budgeting *now* than increasing your income and continuing to live beyond your means.

So rather than deferring debt freedom until you have more money, the power is in your hands to choose to live within your means and start taking steps to pay off debt now.

With that said, we are going to build a budget based on your current circumstances.

How a Budget Can Help You

Your budget gives you a clear snapshot of your finances, and in particular whether you have a surplus or deficit of funds based on your income and expenditure.

It helps you to understand how much you have coming in and going out every month, as well as how much you are spending on fixed and variable expenses. Your budget can also be used to track the progress of debt and savings, if you wish.

A common misconception is that budgets are restrictive as they require us to cap our spending. But everyone, regardless of income, must restrict their spending somewhat to avoid relying on debt.

Even if you earn £1,000,000 each year (and have no savings), your spending must continuously equate to or be less than this to avoid getting in debt. So we must accept that living within our means is an inevitability, whatever our circumstances may be.

I believe that when people use the excuse that budgeting is restrictive as a reason not to start, they really mean that they don't want to cap their spending. They want to spend as much as they want. They want to purchase inconsequentially.

But imagine phrasing these unrealistic aspirations another way: people aren't willing to give themselves financial limits to avoid debt.

They want to chase the hollow happiness of purchasing stuff and sink deeper into unhappiness as they acquire more debt. They want to spend and spend and spend and ignore the stress of the inevitable consequences that this behaviour will guarantee.

When you put it like that, budgeting doesn't seem so bad.

So rather than feeling restricted, see your budget as a financial planner that empowers you to take control of your money and make room for the important things in life. A good budget should:

- Allow you to spend on the things you enjoy, within reason
- Eliminate spending mindlessly on things that don't add value to your life
- Identify areas of overspending, and help to reduce these over time
- Stop you from living beyond your means
- Enable you to allocate surplus income to savings or debt.

How Realistic Is Life on a Budget?

As we get older, we learn that living life too restrictively *or* excessively can have a detrimental effect on our well-being.

Take physical health as an example: you have to find a balance that enables you to feel your best. You have to hydrate, eat and restrict certain foods, exercise and take care of yourself. Occasionally, you might fall off the wagon for a while, but you usually gravitate back towards maintaining a level of physical health that you can live with. If you don't, you pay the price with your health, happiness and well-being.

Conversely, we know that restricting ourselves *too much* can make us feel deprived and overwhelmed. Therefore, we must find a balance between restrictive and excessive to manage our physical health well.

We can apply this exact advice to budgeting. We all have a certain amount of financial resources. We should expect a certain degree of restriction, and in return, we get peace of mind, freedom from the worry of debt, wealth and security.

When we don't stick to our budget, our financial health will waver, financial security will reduce and financial uncertainty will increase. However, if we are too focused on budgeting, we stop enjoying our purchases and what they can bring us.

Therefore, spending requires a balance between *restrictive* and *excessive* for budgeting to work for you.

In the beginning, life on a budget can feel restrictive in comparison to spending excessively, as you might have previously done when getting into debt. However, the aim of your budget isn't to restrict *all* spending, but rather the *unnecessary* spending.

The things that are important to you (within reason) should be budgeted for as normal. But just as you approach your physical health with the expectation that you will reap the benefits by restricting certain aspects of your life, you need to see budgeting in the same way.

Therefore, life on a budget *can* be restrictive, but it's a necessary restriction, particularly if your finances are causing you stress or anxiety.

While it will take a few months of getting used to, I hope that one day, when you start to see your debts reduce during your debt payoff you'll find a little bit of enthusiasm for budgeting.

The Main Elements of Any Budget

There are a few main elements that any budget should have, which are:

- All sources of income, such as:

- Base salary
- Bonuses
- Side hustle income
- Benefits
- Any other forms of income, such as maintenance, one-off payments, etc.
  - Fixed expenses, such as:
- Direct debits
- Bills
- Mortgage/rent
- Routine payments such as internet and mobile phone bills
  - Variable expenses, such as:
- Food
- Entertainment
- Petrol

- Personal spending
- Travel
- Debts
- Savings, such as:
- Saving funds
- Sinking funds

Ideally, you should plan your budget for the month, as most of our expenses occur on a monthly basis, such as mortgage/rent payments.

If any of your income or expenses aren't paid monthly, you can adjust the figures accordingly to reflect your income or expenses on a monthly basis, or you can always plan your budget weekly if you prefer.

So let's get started.

Calculating Your Income

To start building your budget, you need to list all of the details of your monthly income, including:

- Net base salary (the amount that you take home)

- ☐ Bonus payments, expense reimbursements and top up payments from your employer

- ☐ Side hustle incomes

- ☐ Benefits

- ☐ Pension payments (those paid *to* you, not *by* you)

- ☐ Maintenance

- ☐ Any other payments that you receive.

You can use your bank statements as a reference point to ensure that you haven't missed any payments that you receive.

If you are going to compile a monthly budget, every payment that you are paid on a weekly or fortnightly basis should be listed.

If you have any income that is paid as a one-off, annually or less frequently than monthly (for example, a quarterly bonus), do not include these until the month that you will actually receive them.

The reason for this is to build an idea of the income you will have coming in for a particular month, so these payments should only be included on the month you get them. These one-off payments will then carry the advantage that you may not need to apportion them towards livings costs, and you can use them to overpay debts or save as a lump sum.

At the end of this exercise, the income section of your budget should look something like this (with example figures):

Income Source	Amount
Income #1	£1,500
Income #2	£300
Total	£1,800

Calculating Your Expenditure

Now that you've finished calculating your income, let's move on to expenditure. We'll begin with fixed expenses.

- ☐ Fixed expenses

These are the bills that you know are fixed every month. Examples are:

- ☐ Mortgage/rent
- ☐ Direct debits
- ☐ Bills
- ☐ Minimum debt repayments

You might also opt to pay typically quarterly/annual charges on a monthly basis, such as:

- ☐ Council Tax/rates
- ☐ Insurances
- ☐ Gas/electricity (although many of us pay this on a monthly basis as standard)

If you pay this monthly, include the payment every month. If you pay it annually, you will list it as a sinking fund, which is a savings pot for a one-off expense that you will save for routinely every month (we will go into more detail on this later).

Go through your bank account and list every fixed expense that you pay during the month. Remember to also add any bills that you pay in cash.

Additionally, list all of the minimum debt repayments you will make during the month, which you can take from your debt list.

Later, your finished budget will calculate any discretionary income you might have which you can use to make overpayments, but for now, just list the minimum payments.

Compile your list by naming each expense, plus the total and due date, which will make it easy to track when each expense is paid.

List of monthly fixed expenses (with example figures):

Fixed Expense	Total	Due Date
Fixed Expense #1	£100	01/01
Fixed Expense #2	£100	02/01
Fixed Expense #3	£100	03/01
Fixed Expense #4	£100	04/01
Fixed Expense #5	£100	05/01
Fixed Expense #6	£100	06/01
Debt Minimum Payment #1	£100	07/01
Debt Minimum Payment #2	£100	08/01
Debt Minimum Payment #3	£100	09/01
Total	£900	

- Variable expenses

Calculating variable payments is the trickiest part of building your budget. Variable expenses can be difficult to predict, and this is where many of us fail when it comes to financial planning.

Variable expenses are costs that vary depending on your activity. These will be the costs that you apportion money to every month, rather than paying one fixed cost or bill.

Let's take food as an example. Every month, you have the potential to spend money on groceries, takeaways and eating out. Without planning in advance how much to spend on food, you can massively exceed what you can afford. Therefore, having a food budget helps you to keep a figure in mind of how much you should be spending, and will enable you to make informed choices when it comes to your food purchases.

Some of the variable expenses categories that we all use are:

- Food
- Entertainment
- Travel (i.e. petrol, bus and train fares, etc.)

- Personal care (including personal spending, clothing, haircuts, etc.)

- Holidays

Additionally, you will have categories for variable expenses that are personal to you and your circumstances, so add these in here.

Be sensible in your approach; this is where you should consider where you are overspending and how much you can actually afford to spend.

Once you have established your variable expenses categories, start going through your latest bank statement and adding up how much you spent in each of these categories during the previous month, which will give you an idea of how much you need to apportion to each.

Try to remember any cash payments you may have also made to these categories last month, as these are also just as important to consider in getting an accurate representation of what you spend.

It is important to start budgeting by being realistic with your spending. You might be tempted at this point to budget the bare minimum you think you can survive on, in order to maximise your discretionary income.

However, the best way to cut your budget is to do it gradually, which we will go into greater detail on later.

For now, apportion a reasonable amount for each variable expense based on your previous spending and what you think you are *likely* to spend, not what you *aspire* to spend.

List of monthly variables expenses (with example figures):

Category	Total Allocation	Total Paid	Total Left to Pay
Category #1	£100	£0	£100
Category #2	£100	£0	£100
Category #3	£100	£0	£100
Category #4	£100	£0	£100
Category #5	£100	£0	£100
Category #6	£100	£0	£100
Total	£600	£0	£600

Listing this way means that you know your total for the month. Additionally, as you spend throughout the month, you can easily keep track of each category by updating your spending in the 'Total Paid' column and adjusting the 'Total Left to Pay' column.

For example, if you spend £50 in one of the categories above, you will need to adjust your budget accordingly, as follows:

Category	Total Allocation	Total Paid	Total Left
Category #1	£100	£50	£50

Right now, you are just building your budget. But when you are actually *using* it, you will need to keep updating your variable expenses when you spend to keep track of how your financial month is progressing.

Check in with your budget every few days to make sure you capture everything.

Adding Sinking Funds

Sinking funds are saving pots for irregular or one-off expenses, or things that you need to pay for throughout the year that aren't regularly included in your monthly budget.

Not to be confused with emergency savings, sinking funds are where you save for expected expenses. Sinking funds enable you to prepare for irregular costs in advance, so you will no longer use emergency savings or resort to using debt to cover these costs.

You know what you need to pay for over the coming year and this is how you will plan for it. Also, having a sinking fund enables you to spread the cost of a large irregular payment or one-off cost, meaning that you can be consistent in your standard of living every month, without sacrificing a huge chunk of your monthly income to cover a bill.

Here are some common sinking funds:

- Christmas
- Birthdays
- Insurances that you pay annually, such as those for your car or home
- Quarterly/annual bills, such as those for gas or electricity
- Holidays
- Tax, if you're self-employed

- Wedding

- Home deposit or saving for your next home.

This list is not exhaustive so if you have any irregular costs, one-off payments or future plans that you need savings for, include them on your list.

However, during your debt payoff, you will need to be selective when choosing sinking funds because the less you save for, the more money you can put towards debt. Only essential sinking funds should be budgeted for until your debt payoff is complete, after which you will have more money for non-essential sinking funds.

To figure out how much you should save towards your sinking funds each month, you should:

- Estimate the full cost of the sinking fund.

- Divide the cost by the number of months that it covers (for example, if the sinking fund is for an annual cost such as Christmas, divide it by 12. If it's for a quarterly cost such as your gas bill, divide it by 3).

- Build this figure into your budget.

- ☐ Repeat for each sinking fund you have and record them individually in your budget.

List of sinking funds (with example figures):

Sinking Fund	Total to Save per Month
Sinking fund #1	£50
Sinking fund #2	£50
Sinking fund #3	£50
Total	£150

Sinking funds should be used for their intended purpose only. So just as you cannot use your emergency funds for non-emergencies, your sinking funds cannot be used for last-minute purchases or to remedy an overspend in your budget.

Finalising Your Budget

By now, you have all the components you need to finalise your budget. You can do this as follows (using the example figures above):

Total Monthly Income	£1,800	
Total Fixed Expenses	£900	Total Monthly Expenditure = £1,650
Total Variable Expenses	£600	
Total Sinking Funds	£150	
Discretionary Income (Monthly income minus monthly expenditure)	**£150**	

Your total income minus total expenditure is your discretionary income. And by working this out, you've now built your budget!

What to Do With Your Discretionary Income

Hopefully, you will find that you have some discretionary income which you can now use to start building your emergency savings fund if you haven't already got one, or start overpaying debt, if you already have savings.

If this is the case, you can allocate some or all of these funds to a new variable expenses category for emergency savings or overpaying debt.

For example, if you have £150 discretionary income, you can assign this to a category for savings or a debt overpayment in your variable expenses. When you receive your income(s), you can then move this money straight to its assigned pot.

You will notice that apportioning these funds will make your discretionary income figure lower or take it to zero as you are now putting these funds to use. Therefore, you might consider an account buffer, which is a small amount of money in your account that you can use for unexpected expenses that aren't considered an emergency or a sinking fund cost, for example, exceeding your food budget.

While you might be enthusiastic about paying off as much of your debt as possible, remember to be realistic. Sometimes you will go over budget and it's better to have the funds in your account to cover the cost rather than being forced to rely on debt.

What to Do When Your Discretionary Income Is Zero or in a Deficit

This is a surprisingly common scenario – we live in an expensive world, many of us with stagnant incomes, so having no discretionary income is a situation many people are in.

It is important that you don't get discouraged. Remember that the purpose of reading this book is that you are going to take control of your finances, so you are already taking positive action against your problem.

If you have a deficit, you will be able to fix it by trimming your budget or increasing your income, which we will focus on in later chapters.

Building Your Budget: Five Minute Motivation

This Five Minute Motivation is going to help you to see how your financial situation would improve if you had no debt payments to make. You are going to compile a *debt-free wishlist*.

So let's get started:

- ☐ Refer to your new budget and add up your minimum debt repayments.

- ☐ If you have opted to send some of your discretionary income to pay off your debt, add this in too.

- ☐ Total up the figure that you are paying each month, and multiply by 12 to get the total you are likely to spend annually on debt.

- ☐ With this total in mind, compile a list of five things that having this money back in your bank account would enable you to do, have or achieve. Could you:

    - ☐ Go on a holiday every year

    - ☐ Work fewer hours

- ☐ Afford to spend more time at home with your family

- ☐ Pursue a lesser-paid but more fulfilling career path

- ☐ Upgrade your lifestyle or home

- ☐ Afford to treat yourself

- ☐ Help out friends and family

- ☐ Volunteer or give back to others?

☐ Use your debt-free wishlist to drive you. Keep this list somewhere and refer to it regularly, because when you complete your debt payoff, your debt-free wishlist is going to become your new to-do list.

Building a Budget: Recap

In this chapter, you have learned how to build your budget based on your current circumstances.

Building your budget can be daunting; it shows you your exact financial position, which might be worse than you originally thought.

Next, you will work on trimming your budget and increasing your income, both of which you will focus on during the entire span of your debt payoff, and beyond.

These stages are tough, but your hard work will be rewarded by being able to get out debt faster as a result.

Debt Payoff Stage 5: Trimming Your Budget

To trim your budget, you need to decrease your expenses by either reducing their cost or cutting them out of your budget entirely.

When trimming your budget, it is best to take it slowly, tackling one area at a time. If you decide to go cold turkey on your spending, you are likely to find it too difficult to keep up.

Take losing weight as an example; if you drastically cut calories and overtrain, quitting is inevitable. To truly change your habits, changes should be implemented slowly and gradually to have any hope of sustaining long-term success.

When it comes to trimming variable expenses, my advice is to take one category per month and focus on the following:

- What you spent last month

- What you think is a reasonable amount to spend monthly, based on your own circumstances

- The average amount that others spend on this

- How you're going to reduce your spending in this category

- ☐ Any toxic debt behaviour you have that applies to this category and what you're going to do to combat this.

The following month, move on to another category. By this time next year, you'll have completely transformed how you spend *for good*.

You should first focus on trimming fixed expenses, as these are easiest to trim. Then you can tackle variable expenses, as these require a little more focus and hard work. Finally, as you pay off each individual debt, the minimum payment will be trimmed from your budget.

In all three cases, every penny you trim should go towards overpaying debt during your debt payoff.

Trimming Fixed Expenses

Trimming fixed expenses is fairly simple; revisit your budget and trim anything that you don't need, aren't getting value from, could trade for a free version or can happily live without. Is there a gym membership, a subscription service or a financial commitment you can trim?

If you have fixed expenses for things you don't use or can get for cheaper or free, then you should trim these. For example, if you have multiple TV subscription services, you should consider trimming all but the one you use most often from your budget.

For expenses that you are reluctant to trim, consider the *true* cost of what you're paying for. For example, if you have a membership that you only use twice per month, you need to identify the true cost by dividing the monthly cost of your membership by the number of times you use it. If the true cost seems expensive, consider trimming.

Remember that lots of our fixed expenses are bulk-use, such as TV subscriptions and gym memberships. If you aren't using these frequently, you aren't getting value for your money.

As a rule, if you haven't used a service you are paying for in the past two months, you should trim it. You shouldn't pay for something that you aren't using.

When you've trimmed all you can – and remember to inform any service providers of cancellations and downgrades – adjust your budget accordingly.

Trimming Variable Expenses

Trimming variable expenses requires creativity and commitment, but this is where you can also expect to make *huge* savings. While you might need to adapt your approach depending on what you are trying to trim, there is some advice that you can apply to any variable spend.

To start with, consumable products, such as food and hygiene items should *always* be bought from a list (which means that you'll need to plan to buy in advance rather than be influenced when you go into a shop). Do not allow yourself to go into shops or browse online without knowing first what you are there for.

Get into the habit of asking yourself the following questions:

- ☐ Do I need this?
- ☐ Can I afford this?
- ☐ Have I wanted this item for a long time?
- ☐ Will I use it enough to justify the cost?

If you answer "no" to any of the above, you shouldn't buy it.

With shopping, the right money mindset is to prioritise needs over wants and to plan in advance how you'll spend your money. Therefore, there are two major challenges when it comes to shopping in the right money mindset: sales and impulse purchases.

I advise you to avoid sale shopping unless you know what you're buying advance and had planned to buy a sale item.

Sales are a marketing ploy for retailers to offload old stock that was people weren't willing to pay full price for. We are swayed by price, and when we see a discount, we are more likely to relent and buy something. If you wouldn't buy it at full price, don't buy it at half price.

Remember that you save 100% of the purchase price when you don't buy something.

When it comes to impulse shopping, try to identify any toxic debt behaviour you might have. For example, do you impulse shop when hungry? Is there a certain route you take to work that leads you past a few shops that you tend to spend in? Are you in the habit of online shopping at night?

The easiest way to cut out impulse shopping is to not allow yourself to buy anything on the first day you see it. Wait a month after you see the item, and if you're still thinking about it, then you *might* consider buying it.

When it comes to trimming your budget, being able to say "no" will save you thousands of pounds over the course of your lifetime.

This is an approach that will work well with so many variable expenses, such as recreational and social spending, the money you spend on your loved ones and even money you spend on yourself.

Why do we find it hard to say "no"? Many of us find it difficult to talk about money, particularly how much of it we have. We spend a lot of resources projecting the image of ourselves that we want others to see and talking about money – specifically that we don't have enough of it – would ruin that image.

However, you must start to internalise that your own self-perception is more important than the perception that others have of you.

To get into the right money mindset, you should focus on building a version of yourself that *you* can comfortably live with, rather than focusing on how to curate an image that *others* will respond to. Get comfortable with voicing your limits and admitting your finances are finite. Saying "no" to others when you can't afford to do something might result in an uncomfortable exchange, but it'll be a lot easier to sleep at night.

Throughout your debt payoff, you will find ways to cut your current spending by examining where you were going wrong, rectifying toxic debt behaviour and coming up with solutions that enable you to decrease your expenses.

It is important to note that there is no sole solution to lowering your expenditure in every single spending category. That's why I'm not going to advise you to simply "spend less"; of course that's the aim of trimming your budget, but how do you actually achieve this?

The answer lies in adapting your approach to suit each category of your variable expenses. In some categories, you will merely need to take practical steps to trim your spending. In other areas – personal spending, for example – you may need to approach your spending from an emotional perspective to examine your reasons for spending so much on certain things.

There is no "one size fits all" solution to sustainably cut your spending for good, so this is why you need to find solutions that work for *you*. To truly reduce your spending for good without feeling deprived (which may lead to relapse), you need to acknowledge and deal with the fact that, in some areas, your overspending is purely emotive.

A Practical Approach to Trimming Your Budget

There are some variable expenses where a practical approach to trimming will work well. Let's take spending on food as an example.

Food is a common area for overspending. Between groceries, eating out and takeaways, there is a lot of temptation to go over budget.

Start with the amount that you've allocated to food in your budget based on your previous month's spending. How much can you cut this figure by?

If you're overspending, you need to identify the root cause of the problem, which could be:

- ☐ Overbuying groceries
- ☐ Being brand-loyal or only buying luxury branded food
- ☐ Spending too much on takeaways, fast food and eating out
- ☐ Relying on ready meals or pre-packaged foods.

Regardless of the reason you are overspending on food, this is easily fixed through good planning and organisation. Start with a meal plan and compile a shopping list.

Rather than just focusing on dinners, plan breakfast, lunch and snacks, too. Incorporating everything you need for the week in your meal plan will decrease the likelihood of an impromptu trip to the supermarket when you need something.

If you habitually grab lunch on-the-go, plan delicious and easy lunches to rival your pre-packaged go-to. You don't need to resign your Sundays to slaving over Tupperware; a homemade sandwich packed with an easy filling is still a fraction of the cost of a takeaway lunch.

If you find that ready meals are your downfall, you should consider bulk prepping your meals. Bulk prepping allows you to prepare several meals during your downtime and enjoy the same convenience as a ready meal.

You can eat the same meals over a few consecutive nights or bulk prep a few options and freeze portions, to add some variety into your weeknight dinners. And similarly, when you plan dinners, make extra for an easy work lunch the following day.

If you frequently let a moment of weakness turn into a takeaway, plan meals that you will look forward to, using simple recipes and your favourite ingredients.

Your aim is to cook a little more, eat out a little less and give yourself time to go from novice cook to master chef. Stick to meals you enjoy with the aim to learn a new recipe here and there. This gives you the best chance of ditching takeaways and ready meals in the long-term.

As for cutting the cost of your grocery spends, I suggest swapping expensive cuts of meat for cheaper cuts, implementing a meat-free day or bulking out dinners with healthy, fresh vegetables. And instead of planning seven dinners for the week, plan six and have one night per week where you use up all of the leftover items in your fridge and cupboards.

If you previously relied on takeaways and eating out, you might find that the cost of your grocery shopping increases when you start to meal plan and make all of your food at home. But without the need to buy takeaways, lunches on-the-go or fund those spontaneous meals out, you should expect to see *real* savings overall.

Once you have a full shopping list of everything you need for the week, you should aim to buy everything at once, and get out of the habit of popping to the shops more regularly. These little visits are surprisingly expensive, as this is where we pick up the majority of the items we don't need. Besides, you are going to be using the time you would have spent popping to the shops to create fresh and healthy meals.

Trimming your food spending will take time as it requires a change in habits, behaviour and routine, but it is so worthwhile. Not only will you save a fortune by swapping ready meals, eating out, takeaways and pre-packaged food for home cooking, but there are also so many health benefits and sustainable living rewards, too.

But remember, as with budgeting, the key is to find a balance. You might still have the odd takeaway, lunch out or restaurant visit, and that's fine as long as you have these less frequently than before and they are in the budget.

In addition to food, there are many categories in your budget where a practical approach will work.

For example, you can walk instead of using your car or public transport. You can swap expensive date nights, extravagant mate dates and costly days out with the kids to free or low-cost activities. And you can plan a fun staycation instead of an extortionate vacation.

There are so many ways to cut your spending by being practical and creative with your plans.

But how do you deal with emotive spending, which is more about having an urge to do something based on a deeper emotion?

With emotive spending, practical steps will only work for a short time before you might find yourself gravitating towards old habits in search of what you need. In this case, you need to figure out your triggers and put a fix in place that stops them.

An Emotional Approach to Trimming Your Budget

Taking an emotional approach to trimming your budget means knowing your emotional triggers and being willing to fix these – and the underlying behaviour they thrive on – so that you can tackle the problem at the source.

Let's take personal spending as an example, as this is where many people overspend, and spending cannot be trimmed long-term through being practical alone.

If you find that you overspend on personal items, you aren't the only one. Our culture relies on our craving for the next thing to complete us or make us happy, even though we know deep down these are feelings that we cannot attain externally.

But to trim your budget, you need to change the toxic debt behaviour that led you into debt and cut down on your purchases. Sometimes, our purchases are acquired not because we actually want them, but because we want them to compensate for self-perceived deficiencies and inadequacies.

Let's take clothing as an example. Many people gravitate towards expensive clothing brands because they think that by wearing them, others will perceive them as wealthy. However, accruing debt to afford these items moves them further away from wealth, and by buying these things, it reinforces to them that they *need* these items to appear wealthy. This, in turn, lowers self-esteem, which means that they need the boost of others' approval even more, so they keep buying.

This is the cycle of debt – purchasing to feel better, feeling worse, then purchasing to feel better again.

To take an emotional approach to cutting your spending, gain some awareness from your bank statements of the areas in which you are overspending. Examine your toxic debt behaviour and try to pinpoint why you feel the urge to get into debt to achieve something that can never be achieved through purchasing.

Until you confront the underlying motive for your spending, you will continue to spend.

How Much Is Too Much When It Comes to Trimming Your Budget?

Only you will know the true extent to which you can stretch yourself, but I urge you to be realistic when you decide how far you are willing to go. You need to know the difference between the purchases that add value to your life and those that don't serve you.

Many people say that they can't afford to live, when in reality what they mean is that they can't afford to pay for everything they are currently in the cycle of purchasing. But if they were able to identify what they buy that enhances their quality of life and pinpoint the purchases that aren't adding anything but debt, then they could probably afford to live by cutting out the latter.

You will be able to achieve balance in your budget and your life once you figure out the purchases that no longer serve you and remove the guilt of purchasing those that do.

For example, your morning takeaway coffee may be your salvation and you genuinely can't recreate the same at home. In that case, it's fine to buy, as long as it fits into your budget and you've trimmed the purchases that no longer serve you.

By the end of your debt payoff, your budget should reflect your best financial life; not your most frugal or sacrificial life, but the best life you can live that balances purchasing things that make a difference to your quality of life and not purchasing those that add nothing.

However, what if your budget could benefit from an increase in income in addition to trimming your spending? That's what we will focus on next, but first, a Five Minute Motivation to trim your budget.

Trimming Your Budget: Five Minute Motivation

You will be working on trimming your budget over a period of months, particularly with your variable costs, as you come up with a robust plan for cutting your spending and changing your habits. So let's get motivated to start trimming.

For this Five Minute Motivation, you're going to come up with your goal budget. This is the budget that you aspire to have.

We will be looking at what you aspire to cap your spending at every month in each category, regardless of income or debt. Let's call this amount your *goal expenditure*. This means that you'll be taking your fixed and variable expenses and coming up with your goal expenditure for each category.

Then, total up:

- ☐ Your current expenditure

- ☐ Your goal expenditure

Once you have your total current expenditure and your total goal expenditure, answer the following:

- ☐ What's the difference between the two?

- ☐ How many hours per month do you have to work to cover the cost of the difference between these?

- ☐ How much would sticking to your goal budget increase your discretionary income by?

- ☐ What could you use that extra money to pay for?

Use this as your motivation to start trimming.

Trimming Your Budget: Recap

In this chapter, you have learned how to start trimming your budget, and now have a number of different techniques to help you approach this task. While trimming your budget sustainably takes time, allow yourself to focus on this and make it work for you and your life for the long-term.

Debt Payoff Stage 6: Increasing Your Income

While the key to financial freedom is based on living within your means, it is undeniable that most of us could benefit from an increase in income, particularly when we want to make those overpayments.

So, is upping your income an option?

Of course! Many people have a side hustle, which is something they do beyond their day job to earn some extra money.

Using the Right Money Mindset When You Side Hustle

The important thing to note is that a rise in income will only change your circumstances if you've adopted new habits and behaviours that come with being in the right money mindset. If you are still in a "spending" mind frame, then an increase in income will only serve to facilitate more spending. And if your debt is the result of overspending, then the more you earn, the more you'll spend.

A cultural problem we face is the common belief that having money is the answer to any given issue. We are sold the idea of more money, fewer problems. However, given the following two scenarios, which would you choose:

- In scenario A, you win £20,000,000 on the lottery. You spend £21,000,000; some on an expensive house, and the rest is squandered on things that rapidly lose their value, such as clothing, holidays and living beyond your means.
  Your total spend exceeds your winnings. You are starting to realise that you are running out of money, and face losing your home to clear your bills.

- In scenario B, you earn your current income, you spend comfortably less than you earn and you have no debt. Your lifestyle isn't grand, but your family has a home, enough food, basics and the odd luxury item. Christmas and holidays are paid for in advance, and you have a small amount of savings to build on.

Which scenario produces better long-term results?

In scenario A, you have a lot of money but without forming those good habits with spending, you'll still end up in debt. You still have the sleepless nights, worry and anxiety of living beyond your means.

In scenario B, you have a lot less money, but the right money mindset enables you to live free of money worries. You are free to build on your finances. Your family home is intact, and everyone in it has everything they need. Scenario B may be humbler, but it's a much better place to be.

The point is that upping your income won't magically transform your life, particularly when you have unresolved money issues.

However, it is likely that your current income, plus the right money mindset, will. So if you're time poor, choose wisely when it comes to allocating your resources. Don't choose a side hustle that demands so much of your time that you no longer have the ability to stay focused on the right money mindset and the habits that help you form it.

Your debt payoff will benefit more from finding one side hustle that gives you the time to focus on your priorities than signing up for multiple side hustles that leave you overstretched and compromised.

Can't I Just Ask for a Pay Rise or Get a Better-Paid Job?

Successfully completing your debt payoff will result in a major pay rise when you no longer have to make those debt repayments, but are there ways that you could increase your income without having to change your lifestyle right now?

The most obvious solution is to ask for a pay rise at your current job or seek out promotions or other opportunities in your field. Many of us sacrifice higher pay elsewhere for the comfort of our current roles, but if you are serious about increasing your income, this is your simplest option.

However, if this isn't a viable option, then you need to increase your income by taking on a side hustle.

Do I Have to Side Hustle?

If you have a few free hours each week that you can dedicate to making some extra money, why *not* do it? Of course, if you have a deficit in your budget, increasing your income is a necessity, as otherwise, you will be getting further and further into debt each month.

There are other benefits to side hustling that make it an attractive new venture; you can learn new skills and improve your existing skill set or diversify the sources of your income and give yourself more stability. And if you combine your side hustle with a passion, such as by finally writing that book or pursuing the business idea you've had in the back of your mind for a few years, you can make money and do something really fulfilling at the same time.

The Importance of Not Burning Out

Being in the right money mindset and burning out *do not* mix.

Even though side hustling can really make the difference when it comes to paying off debt, remember that there is a finite amount of hours in the day, and you have to know when to stop.

We live in a world that begs you not to sleep; a culture of 24-hour screens and performance-enhancing supplements. It can be confusing when your body is crying out for rest, but your brain craves caffeine, conference calls and continuous scrolling. But remember that your health is much too valuable a price to pay for the sake of shaving a few months off your debt payoff.

I was introduced to the concept of side hustling back when I started my own debt payoff. Suddenly, I went from thinking that my income was capped, to seeing that extra money was abundant and acquiring it was just a matter of swapping my free time for money.

My social media accounts were bustling with people side hustling, and it seemed to be the norm. Quickly, I had a list of several side hustles that I could do to increase my income, and I was all fired up to pay off my debt more rapidly than I had previously anticipated.

I signed up for a number of different side hustles and spread my free time thinly between them. It felt empowering and liberating to take charge of my debt and get a little bit closer to debt freedom.

Soon after, I found that I wasn't as focused on my budget as I'd liked to have been, and I used some of my side hustle money for treats (compensation for losing my free time).

A few weeks into juggling my many endeavours on top of my job, and side hustling started to leave me feeling exhausted.

I quit my cluster of side hustles not long after because they were stopping me from focusing on my debt payoff itself. My sleep had suffered, which made me unproductive. My budget had been neglected, and I was slipping back into old habits of grabbing takeaways when I had no time to cook and pacifying myself with treats when I felt tired and deprived.

It took me about six months to delve into side hustling again, and this time, I picked one thing to focus on and finally found a good balance between downtime and productivity.

The moral of my story is this: the world will tell you to side hustle, and it is up to you to know your limits.

In today's world, endless work ethic is hailed. It can seem that the less you sleep, the more you are admired. Those who "do it all" set the example that the rest of us try to emulate. But the truth is, those who consistently prioritise money-making over their well-being have got their priorities wrong.

So should you side hustle? Ask yourself the following:

- ☐ Do I have the time and energy to commit to this?
- ☐ Will my sleep and well-being still be manageable?
- ☐ Will I still have the right money mindset?

- Will my priorities remain intact?

If you've answered yes to all four, then do it.

Choosing the Right Side Hustle

If you decide to take on a side hustle, focus on one thing that you can really give your time and attention to.

Set criteria that would enable you to side hustle without sacrificing too much balance in your life. For example, if you are introverted and need alone-time, think about what you can do from home that won't leave you feeling that your energy is zapped. If you like to socialise, your ideal side hustle could lie in casual hospitality or retail.

Things to consider are:

- How much time you can commit
- Any current limitations and responsibilities that you need to consider
- How flexible you can be with your working hours
- The realistic rate of pay you want for your time

- How you will counteract the pitfalls of side hustling, such as having less personal time for yourself and your current commitments.

Side Hustle Ideas

Here are some side hustle ideas to get you started:

- Traditional part-time work
    - Restaurant and bar work
    - Supermarket job
    - Delivering takeaways
    - Courier
    - Providing taxi services
    - Seasonal work
    - Overtime
- Working from home
    - Matched betting
    - Selling your used items

- [ ] Purchasing items to resell for profit
- [ ] Making your own bespoke items to sell online
- [ ] Monetised blogging
- [ ] Renting out your spare room
- [ ] Proofreading

- [ ] Phone-based roles
  - [ ] Research and surveys, for example, for government or academic research
  - [ ] Money-making apps
  - [ ] Remote telephone operator

- [ ] Using your expertise
  - [ ] Consultancy work
  - [ ] Tutoring
  - [ ] Translating
  - [ ] Mentoring
  - [ ] Instructing

- ☐ Freelance writing

- ☐ Creating an online course

☐ Starting a business

- ☐ Cleaning

- ☐ Dog walking

- ☐ Babysitting

Increasing Your Income: Five Minute Motivation

For this Five Minute Motivation, you are going to examine the impact the right side hustle will have on your budget. So here goes:

- ☐ Pick a side hustle from the list of ideas (you can also choose another idea you had in mind).

- ☐ Estimate out how many hours you can commit to your side hustle each month (remember to be realistic).

- ☐ Do a quick bit of research on the average rates of pay for your side hustle and figure out how much you can expect to make per month based on the hours you are able to commit to it.

- ☐ Plot this figure into your budget temporarily and see the difference that it makes. How much better off will you be? If you were previously in a deficit, does this solve it? Or how many months will it shave off your debt payoff?

Use this for inspiration to see what you can achieve when you get started.

Increasing Your Income: Recap

In this chapter, we have covered increasing your income and what to look out for when you choose a side hustle. By now, you'll have an idea of whether or not you will be able to take on a side hustle, and what you should expect if you decide to go for it.

Debt Payoff Stage 7: Saving for Emergencies

Having a small pot of emergency savings is the foundation for your successful debt payoff. It prepares you for unexpected expenses that might crop up at a time when you are going to be allocating all of your spare income towards your goal of debt freedom.

During your debt payoff, your emergency savings are key to helping you remain focused on your goal without having to change your plans or get back into debt if something unexpected occurs (and nothing kills momentum on your debt payoff like going further into debt).

Your emergency savings help to reduce:

- Unexpected expenses in the event of an emergency
- Feeling anxious over money
- Financial insecurity.

Your emergency savings help you to:

- Form good financial patterns and improve money management

- Learn how to have savings without spending them unnecessarily

- Build future wealth and increase your financial net worth

- Get into the right money mindset.

So why do you need emergency savings? In the case of an emergency, can't you just fall back on debt?

Well, let's say you do. Let's take an example that your car breaks down during your debt payoff. You have no savings, and you need to put the cost of repairs on your credit card. You need to pause your debt payoff, which will affect how long it'll take to pay off your debt *and* it'll have an impact on your budget.

All that momentum is lost. You risk losing the right money mindset by going backwards in your debt payoff. You get demotivated when some of your hard work is undone. Your sole goal is to get out of debt, and you find yourself relying on it again and repeating old patterns.

However, if you had emergency savings, you could pay for your car repairs without pausing your debt payoff. Momentum and motivation remain as is. You get a boost from having savings to take care of life's crises. You reap the success of your hard work, and finally see the benefit of the new patterns you are in.

Your right money mindset is not only intact but enhanced by your ability to solve your financial problems.

That's why you should build emergency savings before paying off debt. It's so important that, right now, this is the highest your debt will ever be. So you need emergency savings to facilitate this, thereby ensuring you are never reliant on debt again.

Your debt payoff hinges on focus, motivation, momentum and the right money mindset. You need to prepare in advance to give yourself the best chance of achieving your goal.

What Do Emergency Savings Cover?

Emergency savings can be used to pay for unexpected emergencies *only*, which include:

- ☐ Unexpected home repairs and replacement of essential items

- Unexpected essential car repairs
- Unexpected medical/dental bills
- Bills and household costs in the event of an unexpected drop in income.

Examples of expenses that cannot be funded by emergency savings are:

- Christmas and birthdays
- Routine or advance-planned medical/dental treatments
- Budgeting fails
- Impulse purchases
- Non-essential repairs/replacements
- Holidays.

For some of these expenses, we use sinking funds rather than emergency savings.

How Much Should My Emergency Savings Be?

The total of your emergency savings should be enough to cover the cost of a few unexpected expenses, but not large enough that it makes you complacent with your finances by providing a financial cushion for non-emergencies.

I recommend taking one month's basic expenses (e.g. mortgage/rent, essential bills and basic food and living costs) as a starting point, then consider some of the following, in case adjustments are needed:

- Your current living situation
- Your monthly living costs
- The average cost of living in your area
- How much you could afford to live on if you lost your current income, and for how long.

Only you will truly know how much need.

In my own debt payoff, my emergency savings were £1,000. I opted for this figure because it was large enough to cover a real emergency and small enough that it wouldn't cover reckless spending. But that was based on my own circumstances, and emergency savings don't abide by a "one-size-fits-all" approach. So if you think you need less or more, then work out your numbers and adjust accordingly.

Funding Emergency Savings When You Already Have Savings

We are culturally encouraged to build savings, but at the same time, it is acceptable to have debt. But is that the right money mindset? Does it make sense to add to your savings each month while continuing to accrue debt?

No. Not even a little bit.

Let's look at savings and debt in terms of your net worth. If you have £5,000 in savings and £10,000 in debt, your net worth is -£5,000. That means that in real terms, you are £5,000 in debt overall.

Let's look at savings and debt in terms of interest. If you have £5,000 in savings and £10,000 in debt, you will typically earn between £50 and £100 in annual interest on savings, and you can typically pay upwards of £500 in annual interest on debt. Why pay more to borrow money that you already have?

And lastly, let's look at savings and debt in terms of the right money mindset.

We tend to think that having savings provides a safety net in case of an emergency. Therefore, we prepare for emergencies by having savings. At the same time, we see debt as an accepted risk, although we know having debt makes us vulnerable in case of an emergency. So what we have is savings as a safety net and debt that cancels out our safety net.

At the beginning of your debt payoff, the right money mindset may need to be fuelled by a little bit of fear. You need to look at debt as a threat to your stability and use any excess savings you have to decrease it. This will reduce your savings, which in turn will change how you view them. No longer will your savings be a financial cushion, but a basic fund for emergencies only.

If you use your savings to pay off debt and only keep a small fund for emergencies, your net worth will remain the same and your interest charges will dramatically reduce, but most importantly, your debt figure will shrink, and your lowered savings will provide the fuel to take charge of your finances once and for all.

Paying off your debt with excess savings is a great investment to kickstart your debt payoff. Trust me on this.

Where to Keep Your Emergency Savings

Your emergency savings should be easily accessible in case of an emergency, without being kept where you can access them on impulse, so that you won't be tempted to dip into it for anything other than emergencies. I suggest an account that:

- ☐ You don't hold a debit card for, so you can't easily access the funds for everyday spending

- ☐ You need to physically make contact with the holding bank to move funds, therefore making it as hard as possible to access your money

- ☐ You can't rhyme off the details of, in the case of an online shopping "emergency" (we've all been there).

How Do I Start to Save for Emergencies?

Now that you have a budget and are working on reducing your expenses and increasing your income, building emergency savings is a quick milestone to achieve rapidly.

You should take as much as possible from your discretionary income each month until your emergency savings pot is fully funded. Then you can move on to overpaying debt, which we will cover next.

Saving for Emergencies: Five Minute Motivation

This Five Minute Motivation focuses on deciding how much your emergency savings should be.

Think back over the past two years and take a quick note of all emergencies during that time.

Think of real emergencies rather than times where you impulse shopped or had to cover the cost of a planned event, such as a birthday or Christmas. Think of times where your car needed an emergency repair, or when something important at home needed fixing or replacing.

Add up the total and consider this as the basis for your emergency savings. Adjust if needed, based on the recommendations from the *How Much Should My Emergency Savings Be* section.

I suggest opting for the bare minimum to fund your emergency savings pot, but not so little that you won't be able to cover the cost in the event of an actual emergency. Think of a figure that provides comfort without making you *too* comfortable.

Saving for Emergencies: Recap

In this chapter, we've covered building your emergency savings, as well as how to get into the right money mindset when it comes to savings.

By now, you should know the amount that you need to save in order to complete your emergency savings fund. If you have excess savings, you will know how much you will use to reduce your debt total, which is a fantastic start to your debt payoff.

Debt Payoff Stage 8: Overpaying Debt

Now that you're motivated and have the right mindset, you're dealing with any toxic debt behaviour, you have your debt list, you're budgeting, working on trimming your budget, increasing your income and have some funds set aside for emergencies, it's time to overpay debt.

While this will be a long journey, there is little to say other than: *keep going*. Every month, you'll apportion the most you can afford to reducing your debt total. You'll be motivated as you tick off each debt and move on to the next. As you pay off a debt, you can then allocate the money you would have otherwise spent servicing that debt to overpay more debt.

Paying off debts and using the money that it frees up in your budget to pay more off your debts is known as a *debt snowball*. Combining this with reducing your expenses and upping your income, your snowball will turn into an avalanche.

Figuring Out Your Debt-Free Date

By now, you'll have an idea of how much you can expect to put towards overpaying debt every month, which enables you to figure out your *debt-free date*, i.e. the day you can officially jump with joy, knowing that you'll never have to make another debt repayment again.

To work out your debt-free date:

- Add up your minimum monthly debt repayments, plus your expected monthly overpayment, to get your total monthly debt payment.

- Divide your total debt by your monthly debt payment.

- The figure you get is the number of months it will take you to repay your debt. Use this number to figure out the date that you will be debt-free.

You may have to consider interest charges as they will have a bearing on your debt-free date. However, you will find that your debt-free date may change several times over the course of your debt payoff as your circumstances change over time. You may miss the odd overpayment or find that you can make higher overpayments as you trim your expenses and increase your income.

The main thing to remember is that you now have a date to work towards, and you know in general terms how long you should expect your debt payoff to last.

Paying Off Debt Is a Marathon, Not a Sprint

Paying off debt can be slow, and you might find yourself feeling impatient, deprived or frustrated. The actual payoff is the hardest part of your journey. There will be times when you get demotivated or feel like quitting.

That's when you need to go back and revisit the motivational techniques in this book. Re-evaluate the reasons for your debt payoff often and keep aligning them with what's motivating you.

Make yourself promises of how you'll be rewarded when your debt payoff is complete. Direct your frustration from your debt payoff to your debt itself and use it as fuel to keep striving for debt freedom.

I urge you to allow yourself to feel proud of your debt payoff and to talk about it. Keeping it secret means you'll never feel as accountable as if you were telling people about your efforts. Reach out and find a community, even if it's through social media, as I did. You'll be amazed at how it can help.

Remember to seek out the benefits from your debt payoff during your journey. Notice the little things, like a better night's sleep, less stress and an appreciation of what you already have, rather than lusting after objects for sale that falsely promise to improve your life. Enjoy the feeling of accomplishment you'll get from watching your debt decrease.

And finally, celebrate each step and every milestone along the way. Your debt payoff duration is made up of little fragments; moments of inspiration, days of hard work, a willingness to continue even when it feels too hard and the drive to take charge of your financial future. Each of these is a component of your overall success.

So no matter what, always clap for yourself.

Overpaying Debt: Five Minute Motivation

For this Five Minute Motivation, you are going to look ahead at the milestones you should expect now that you know your debt-free date.

Let's split your debt payoff into quarters and figure out how much you should expect to shave off your debt by the end of each quarter. To do this:

- ☐ Figure out, using your debt-free date, when you'll be one quarter, one half and three-quarters of the way through. Write down these months on one side of your page.

- ☐ Figure out, using your debt total, three quarters, one half and one-quarter of your debt. Write them on the other side of the page.

- ☐ Use these figures to motivate you to see how much progress you'll make over time.

Breaking your debt payoff into chunks gives you little milestones along the way and helps to make the task feel less overwhelming. Use these milestones to remind yourself that your goal is long-term, but your progress in paying off debt is achieved *as soon as you make an overpayment*.

Overpaying Debt: Recap

In this chapter, we have covered the process of overpaying debt and figured out your debt-free date.

Everything you need to know to achieve success has been covered in the previous chapters, and you know it all now. You are armed with everything you need to pay off your debt. Now it comes down to making overpayments, being patient and staying in the right money mindset until you complete your goal. So keep going until you are debt-free!

Life After Debt

Whether you are reading this before you start your debt payoff, or you're revisiting this chapter after you've achieved your goal, let me just say that life after debt is such a great place to be.

Debt freedom affords you the right to get paid without having to factor in the cost of paying off your previous purchases for several years. You've given yourself a pay rise of the sum of your minimum debt repayments, and then some.

With the right money mindset, you might find that you have even more discretionary income each month now that your income isn't being engulfed by unnecessary purchases, and your focus is on how to live your best financial life.

Money aside, what other life enhancements does debt freedom offer you? Are you sleeping better and stressing less? Are you able to focus more on what's important? Have you learned through your debt payoff what's important to you? Are you able to cut your working hours or finally leave that job you hate?

When you don't have money dictating your decisions, life after debt opens up a world of possibilities.

It is my hope that despite the challenges that came with your debt payoff, you enjoyed achieving what you set out to. If so, keep the momentum going and set a new financial goal.

Where Do You Go From Here?

After completing your debt payoff, you should have a lot more money in your pocket every month that used to be eaten up by debt. You should have a great understanding of how to budget and manage your money. You are focused on the right money mindset. You've finally kicked that toxic debt behaviour that was holding you back.

Your financial future is in your hands and it's up to you where to go from here: overpaying your mortgage, building savings, paying off student loans, investing . . . anything is possible.

Whatever you've got planned for after your debt payoff, this is your new beginning. Make your debt payoff pay off for you, and start building your best financial life from here on in. You've done the hard work and you deserve it.

I'm sure you'll agree that paying off debt is money well-spent.

Debt Payoff FAQs

There are a few frequently asked questions that have cropped up time and time again, both on my own debt payoff journey and when supporting many others. Here are those debt payoff FAQs.

Should I combine my money with my partner's money?

In your relationship, you and your partner might combine your money, or keep your finances separate. Perhaps you combine your money to have more security should either of you lose your job. Perhaps you don't combine your finances to remain financially independent.

Regardless, you have opted to do so for a reason. And whatever the reason, you've chosen it because it works best for you, and that is *your choice to make*.

If you combine your finances, then your budget should include all incomes, expenditures, debts and savings together, so that you can get a clear idea of your overall financial picture.

If you don't combine your finances, you can still maintain one budget. You can list incomes, expenditures, debts and savings together. This will help you to identify the amounts that each of you are contributing to your household and figure out a fair way of apportioning joint payments and paying joint debts. It might be a little more complex but maintaining a joint budget while still keeping your finances separate will enable you to work towards your debt payoff together.

<u>How can I get my partner on board?</u>

Often, the idea of debt freedom starts with one fired-up partner who persuades the other to start tackling the problem together. Your partner could be as enthusiastic as you, or they may be resistant to the debt payoff because they aren't triggered by the same things.

So how do you get your partner on board? Here are some techniques and strategies that might persuade them:

- ☐ Your partner will need an incentive that speaks to them. Remember, different people are incentivised by different things. For example, you might be driven to pay off debt by the stress that your debt is causing you, whereas your partner may not feel stressed out about debt. Therefore, you need to adapt your approach.

Think of what drives your partner and use that as a motivator to get them on board.

- If your partner is unwilling to sacrifice their current lifestyle in order to pay off debt, take this into consideration when building your budget. Listen to your partner's concerns and why they aren't willing to give up certain things, and if possible, try to build some of these into your budget to ensure your partner doesn't feel deprived.

- Perhaps your partner would prefer to bury their head in the sand when it comes to debt, and you are having difficulty in making them realise the problem. In this case, you need to start making debt more of a focal point in your relationship without making your partner feel overwhelmed (which is often the reason they are unwilling to face the issue). Have open discussions about your debt and instead of storing your bank statements away, pin them somewhere prominent. Making debt a topic of normal conversation can bring your partner back to reality.

Regardless of the strategy you take, you need to communicate clearly and concisely with your partner and focus on how to move forward at all times.

Rather than dwelling on their unwillingness to pay off debt, which can spiral into frustration and arguments, try to understand their reluctance and use this to persuade them to come around.

You might find that you will have to begin your debt payoff alone and lead by example to highlight the benefits of paying off debt to your partner. It may take some time, but when your partner realises the financial benefits of paying off debt, it will become more attractive for them to come round to your way of thinking.

Or perhaps you've tried everything, and your partner still isn't on board. In this case, tackle only the debts in your name (i.e. sole debts and joint debts that you are party to). Remove your partner's sole debts from your debt list. You are doing both of you no favours by paying off debts that aren't yours.

While this may feel like a strain on your journey, the one thing you must do is *continue*.

I'm single / have kids / am on a low income – can I do this?

Absolutely!

I include this question due to the sheer volume of people out there who believe that only people with certain lifestyles or advantages can pay off debt.

In my own debt payoff, my partner and I earned average salaries. We didn't get any financial help from outside sources, and we aren't from privileged backgrounds. The secret to our debt payoff was that there was no secret; it was a combination of budgeting, decreasing our expenses, a small amount of side hustling and continuously making debt overpayments.

So regardless of your circumstances, as long as you can make overpayments, you can follow this plan.

This might require increasing your income or cutting your expenses, which depends on your personal circumstances, but it's never a matter of *can* or *cannot*, but always a matter of *how* and *by when*.

I encounter a lot of people who doubt their ability to pay off debt before they've even tried. Contrary to their belief that they can't pay off debt due to circumstance, the only thing standing in their way of debt freedom is their mindset. You need to believe that you can do it to start putting a plan of action in place, which will get results.

Remember, whether you think you can or you can't, you're right.

<u>Should I consolidate debt?</u>

If you are considering consolidating debt, you will need to understand your motive for this in order to decide if it's the right course of action.

If your motive is genuinely related to saving money – for example, if your debts are accruing significantly more interest individually than as a consolidation – this might be a good idea.

However, if your motive lies in thinking this will fix your issues, *don't* consolidate. We are taught that consolidating debt is financially savvy, and many people consider it the answer to their debt problems. But it doesn't decrease your debt, it just lumps it together.

Detrimentally, consolidating can change your mindset by removing your drive to pay off debt. The feeling of urgency that triggered your debt payoff is necessary; it's going to drive you to get beyond your comfort zone and start making overpayments. If consolidating puts you back in your comfort zone by providing a hollow solution, it's not worth it.

Plus, it's oh-so-satisfying ticking off those debts one by one when you don't consolidate.

In short, only consolidate if it *doesn't* solve the problems that pushed you to want to get out of debt. You're going to need those problems to keep you motivated throughout your debt payoff.

What resources are there to help me during my debt payoff?

There are so many ways that you can reach out for support or create your own support networks while paying off debt. Here are my recommendations:

- ☐ Have an accountability partner that knows your goals and isn't afraid to tell you when your actions aren't aligning with them.

- Keep a diary to track progress and have a place to vent when things get tough. This will allow you to process your emotions and help with potential burn-out.

- Visualise your progress. You can do this by creating a visual representation of your debt and updating it as and when you make a payment.

    Many people use a "printable" for this, which is a picture of something that symbolises each debt that you can colour in when you've hit a milestone. For example, if you are paying off a £5,000 car loan, you can use an outline of a car, with the image separated into ten sections. For every £500 you pay off, you get to colour in a section.

    Printables sound basic, but they are a great motivator because they really help to show how your progress is paying off.

- Find a community of like-minded people on social media, online or in real life. This will help with feelings of isolation on your debt payoff.

    When I first started my debt payoff, I created an account on social media to hold myself accountable and found my tribe in the process. My social media account became a lifeline for my goal, because nothing keeps you motivated like a group of people on the same path. Finding a place where everyone understands your challenges and celebrates your triumphs can be a huge motivator.

What's better: an electronic or paper budget?

It's entirely up to you. Electronic is easier, in my opinion, but there is something really satisfying about keeping your budget in a notebook where you can physically tick off paid expenses. Regardless, use what you're most comfortable with.

Good luck!

Acknowledgements

The hard work that went into this book could never have happened without the support of the people around me. I would like to say thank you to my husband, Ryan, who is my biggest cheerleader in everything I do.

To Leon- you weren't even born when I wrote this book but I really hope it inspires you some day to see that you can do whatever you want to do.

To my friends and family, thanks for all of your support and being the greatest circle a girl can have.

To everyone out there online posting transparently about their debt journeys, thank you for all you do. You inspired me, kept me sane and pushed me to articulate all of the ideas rustling about in my brain.

A special thanks goes to my dog, Jesse, who got up every morning at five A.M. to sit at my feet while I wrote this book. I know you were probably just making it known that you wanted to go out for a walk but our morning ritual kept me going!

Disclaimer

This content of this book should not be considered as financial advice. Please conduct your own research or seek independent financial advice if and when required.

Copyright

All rights reserved. No part of this book may be reproduced or modified in any form, including photocopying, recording, or by any information storage and retrieval system, without permission in writing from the publisher.

Published by Grainne McNamee © 2019 Belfast, Northern Ireland

Version 11.0

Printed in Great Britain
by Amazon

28437923R30088